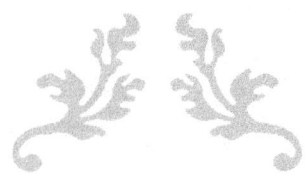

MANDALAS FOR THE
WORK PLACE

Stephinie R Johnson

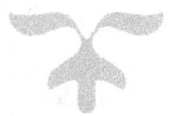

Mandalas for the Work Place

Man-da-la

Noun

- A symbol in a dream, representing the dreamer's search for completeness and self-unity.

Mandalas are a Hindu or Buddhist geometric pattern representing the universe. Mandalas are a tool used to aid in meditation. It relaxes the mind of those who either draw or color the shapes. Many therapists have incorporated the use of mandalas into their sessions as a form of coping mechanism.

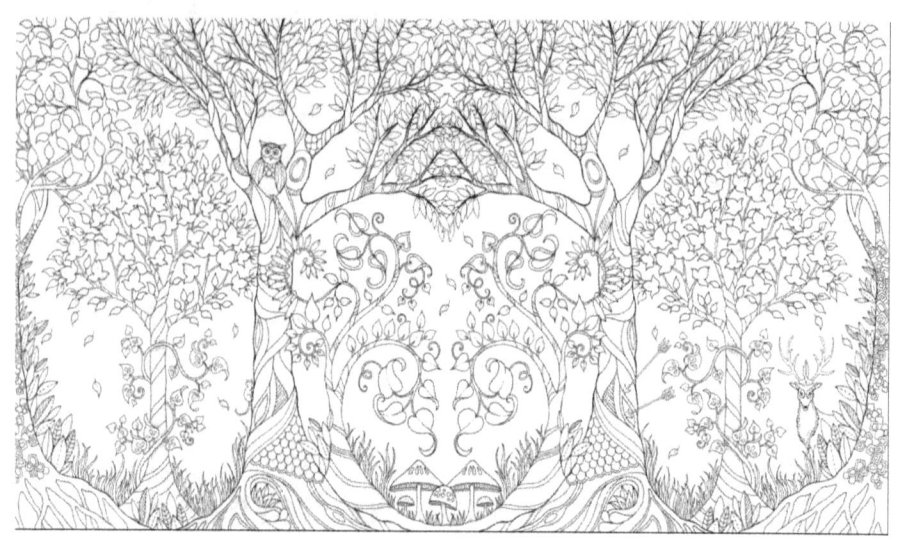

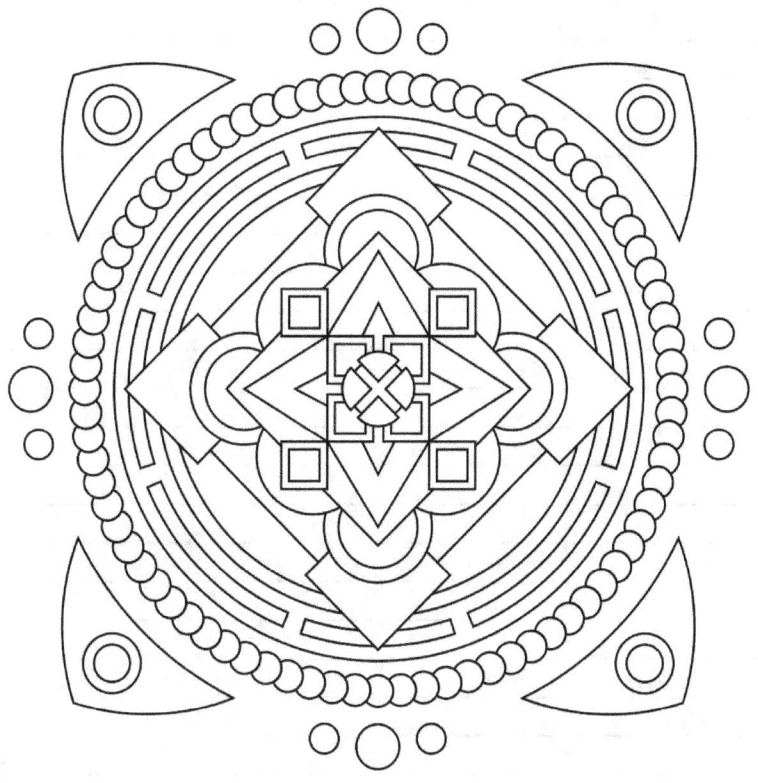

"Set peace of mind as your highest goal, and organize your life around it." Brian Tracy

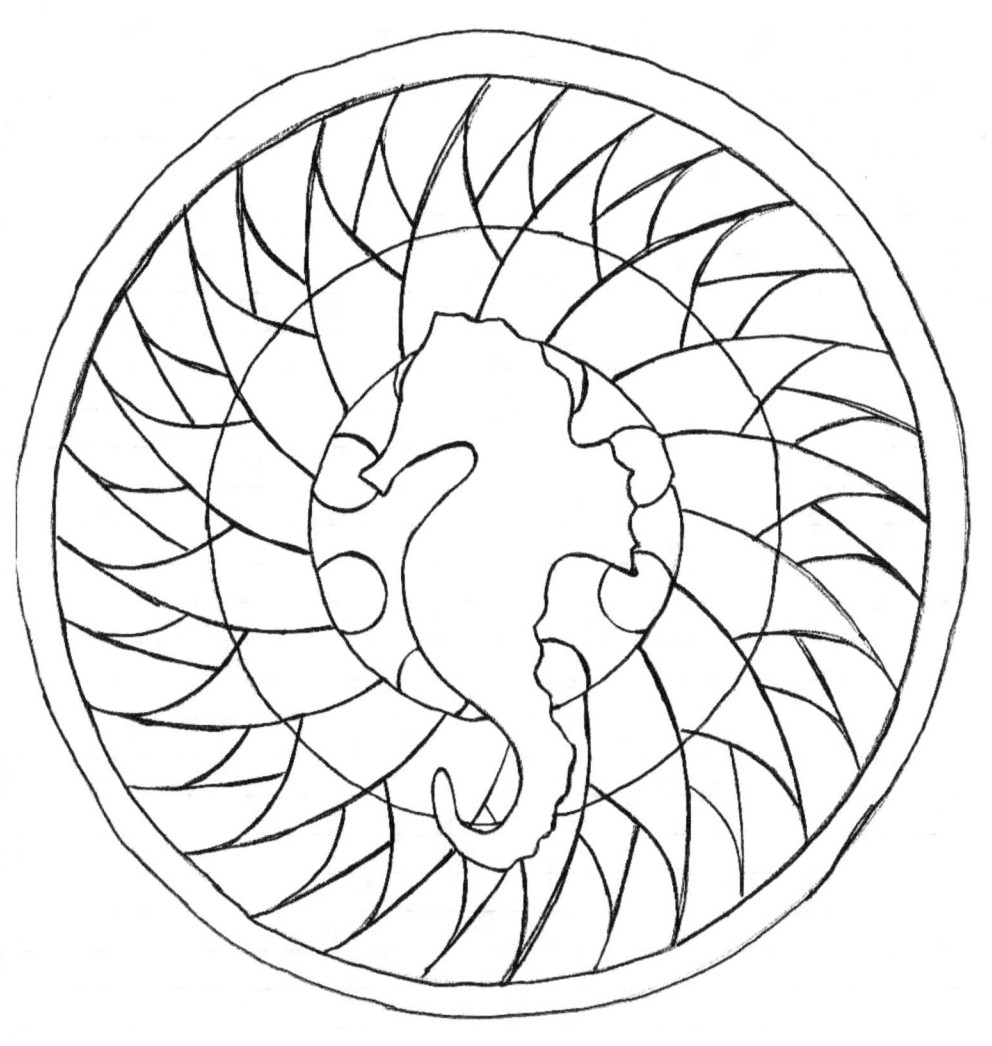

"Maturity is learning to walk away from people and situations that threaten your peace of mind, self-respect, values, morals or self-worth." Anonymous

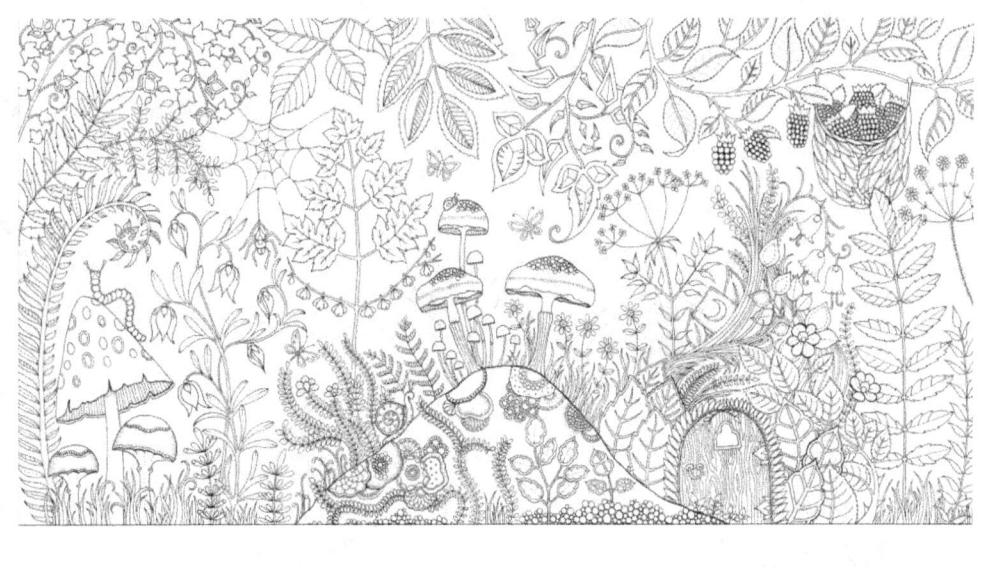

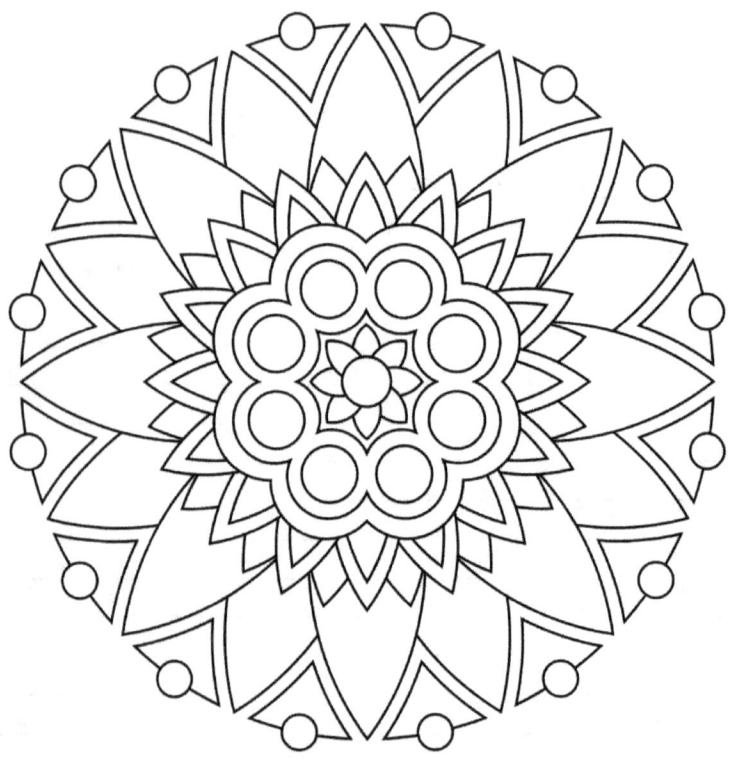

"Nothing is more conducive to peace of mind than not having any opinion at all." Georg C Lichtenberg

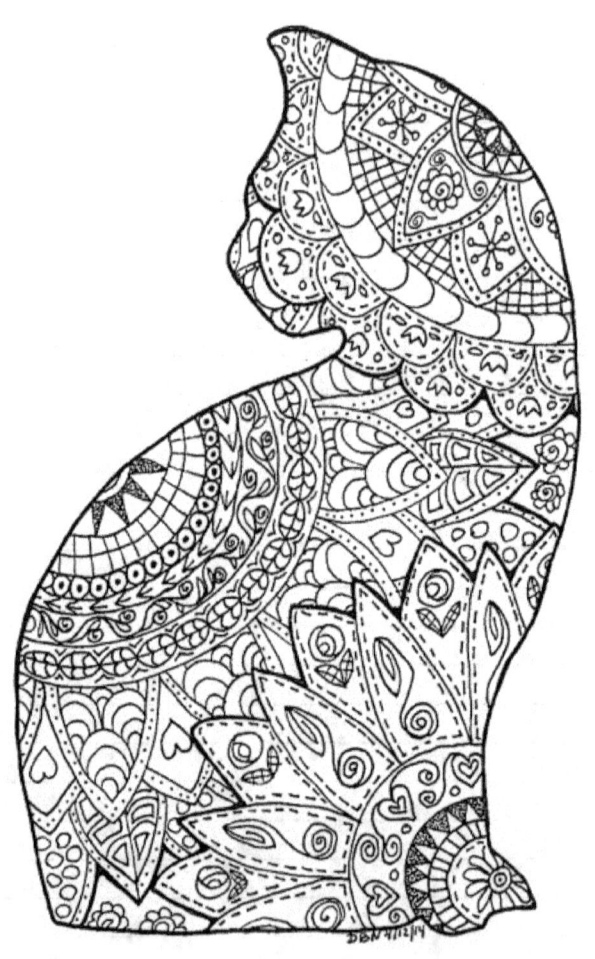

"There is a wonderful mythical law of nature that the three things we crave most in life — happiness, freedom, and peace of mind — are always attained by giving them to someone else." Peyton C. March

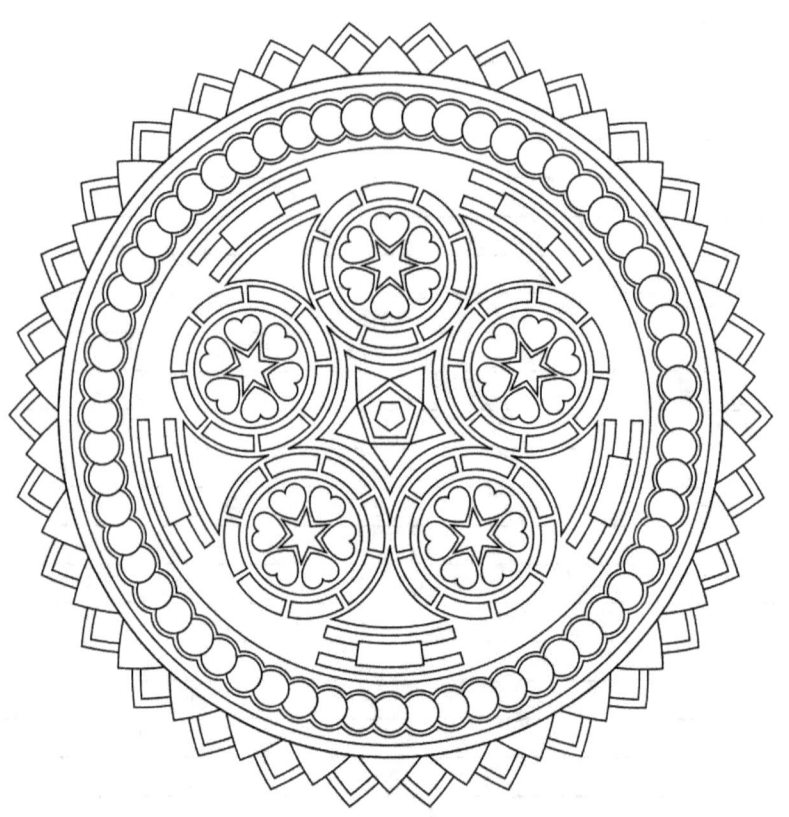

"Peace of mind is clearly an internal matter. It must begin with your own thoughts and then extend outward. It is from your peace of mind that a peaceful perception of the world arises." Anonymous

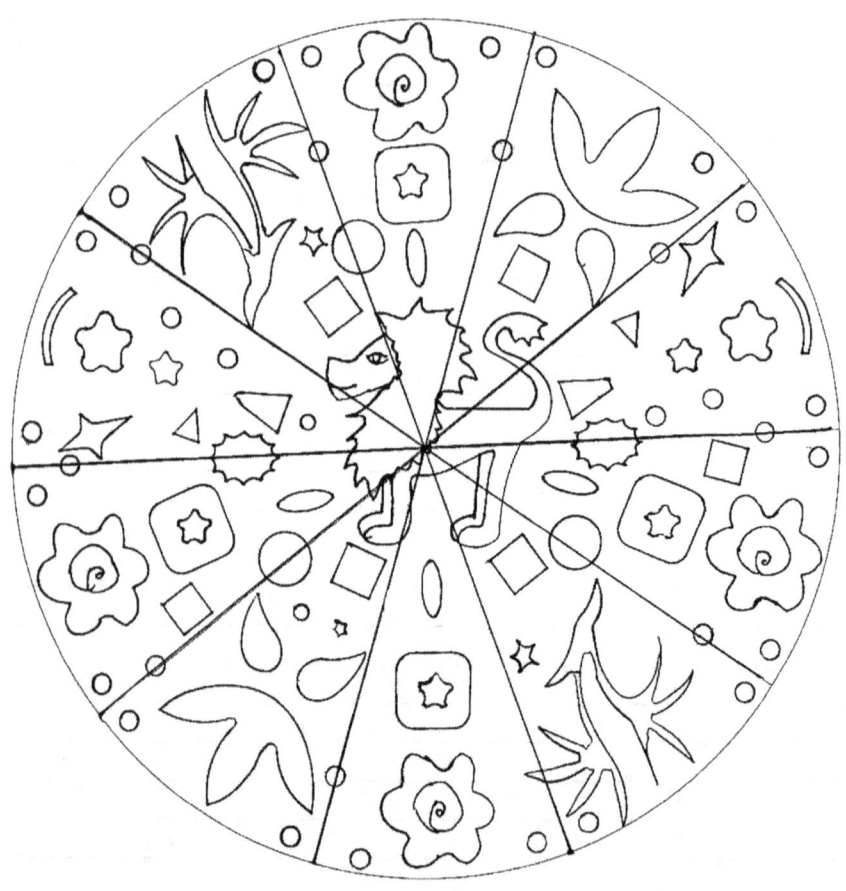

"You can have peace of mind, improved health and an ever-increasing flow of energy. Life can be full of joy and satisfaction." Norman Vincent Peale

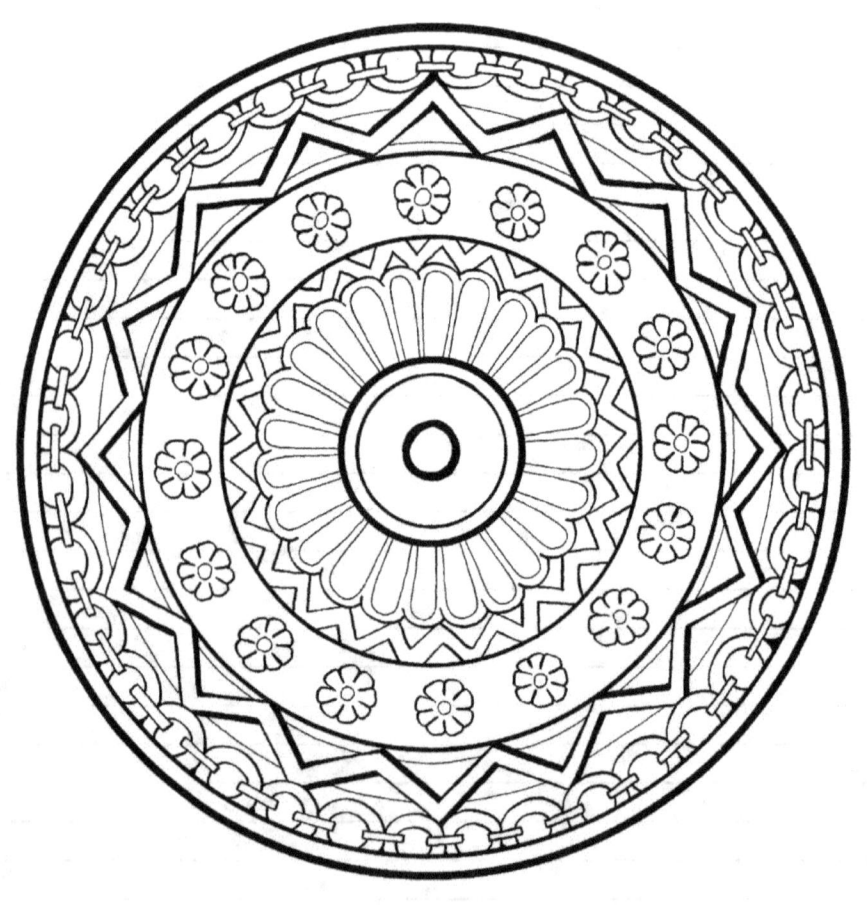

"Nothing can bring you peace but yourself." Ralph Waldo
Emerson

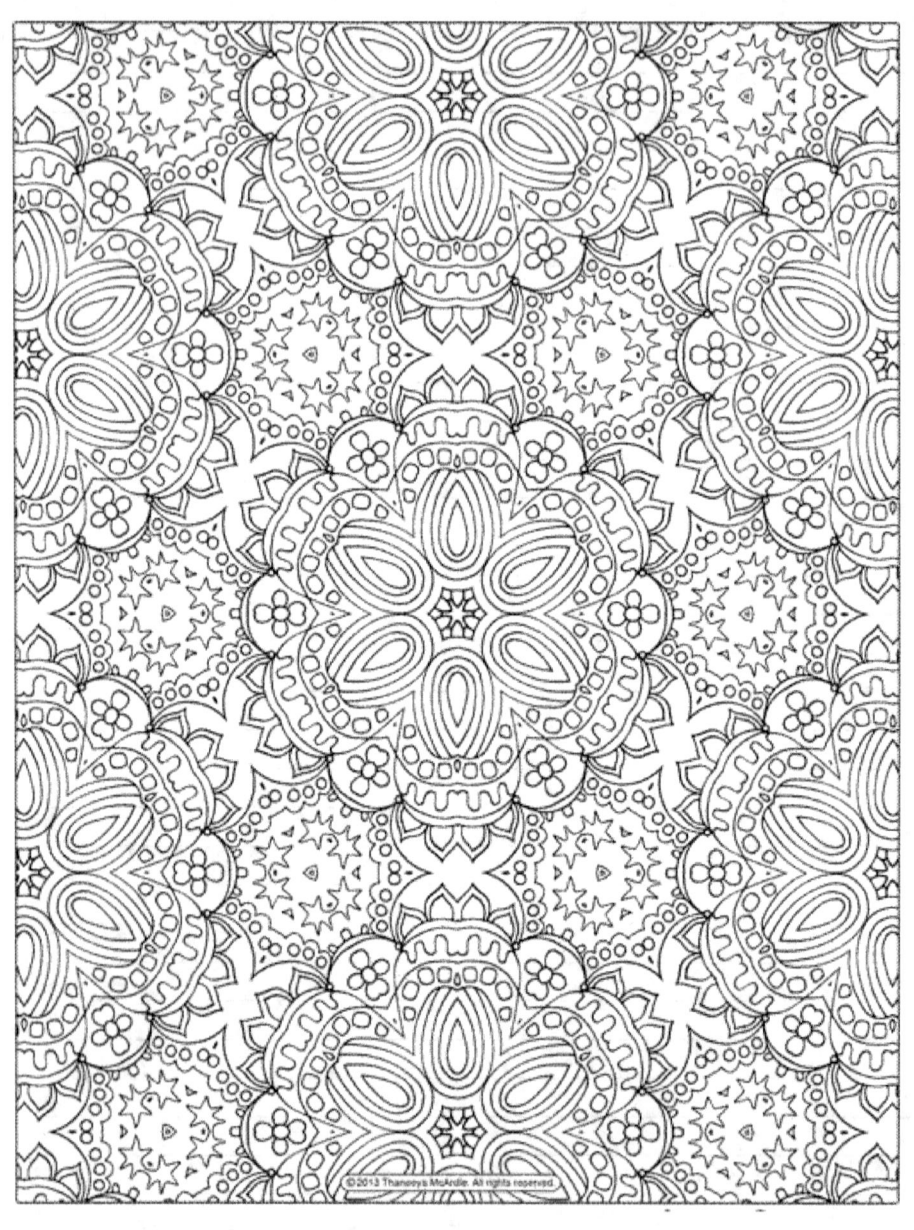

"Peace of mind comes from not wanting to change others."
Gerald Jampolsky

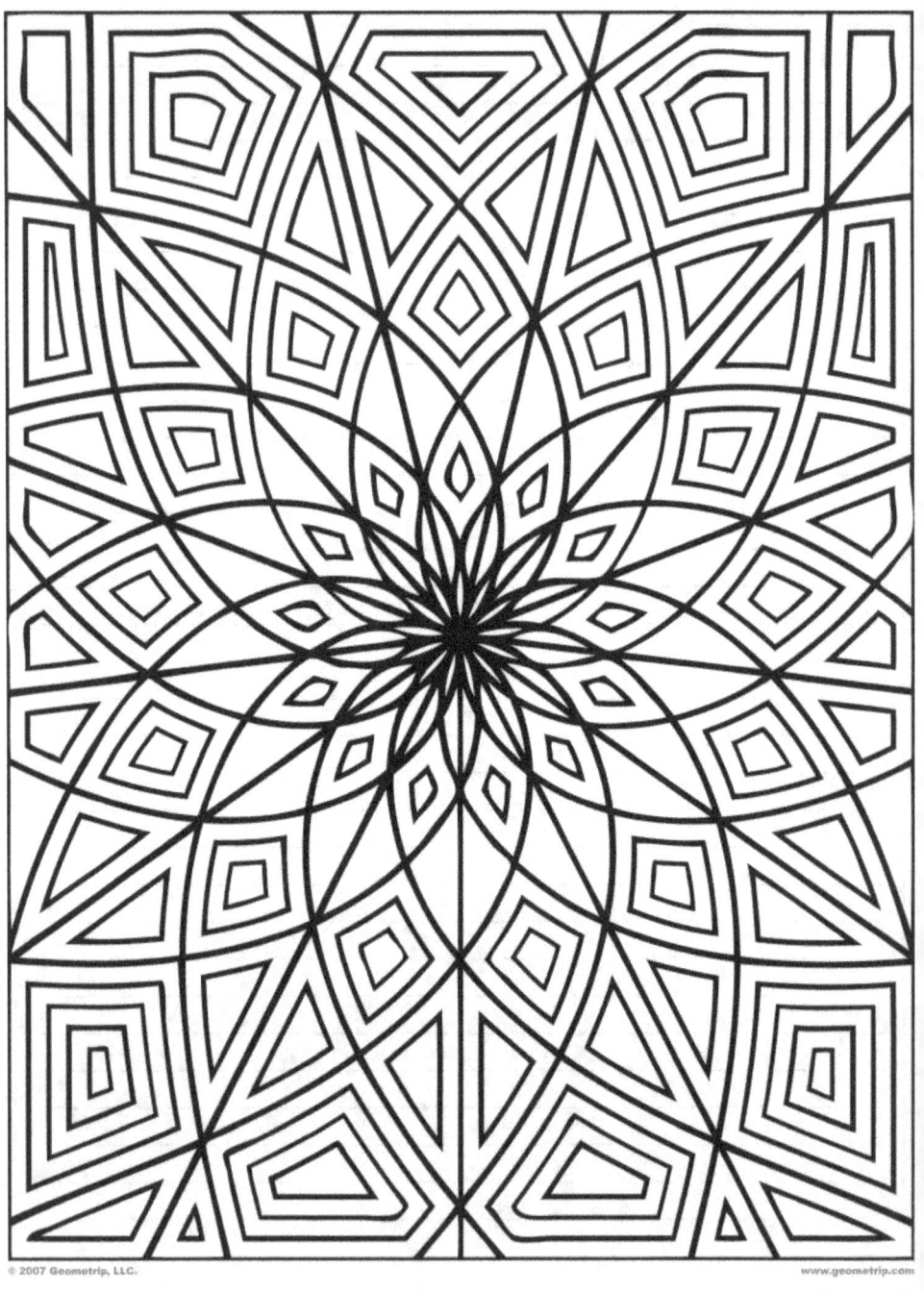

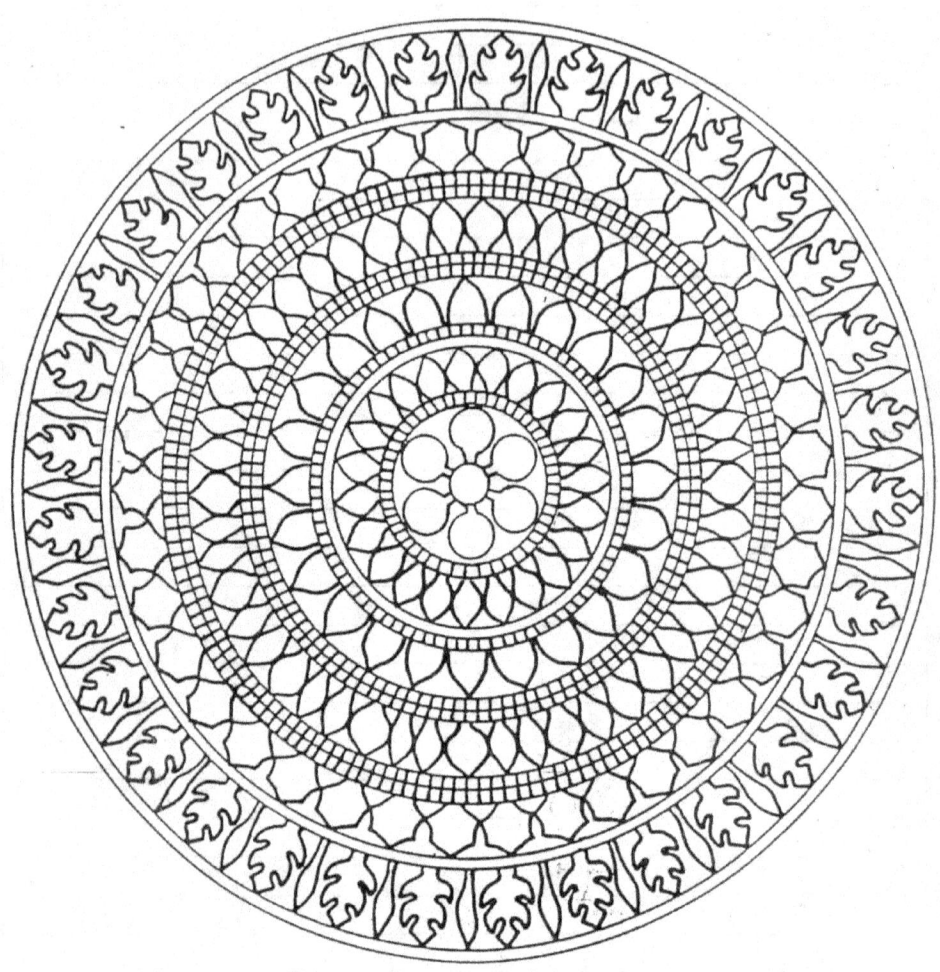

"Promise yourself to be so strong that nothing can disturb your peace of mind. To talk health, happiness, and prosperity to every person you meet. To make all your friends feel that there is something in them." Christian D. Larson

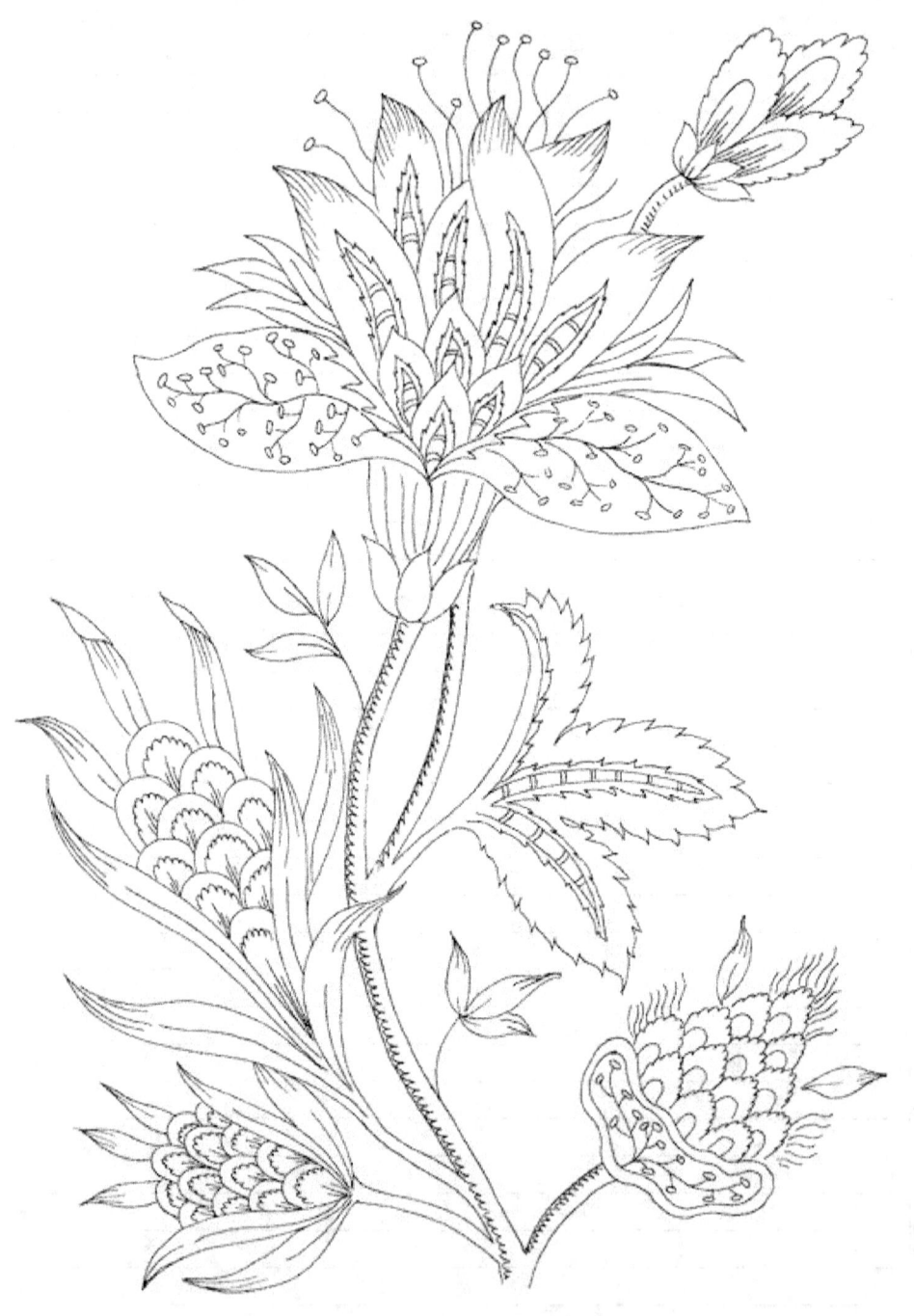

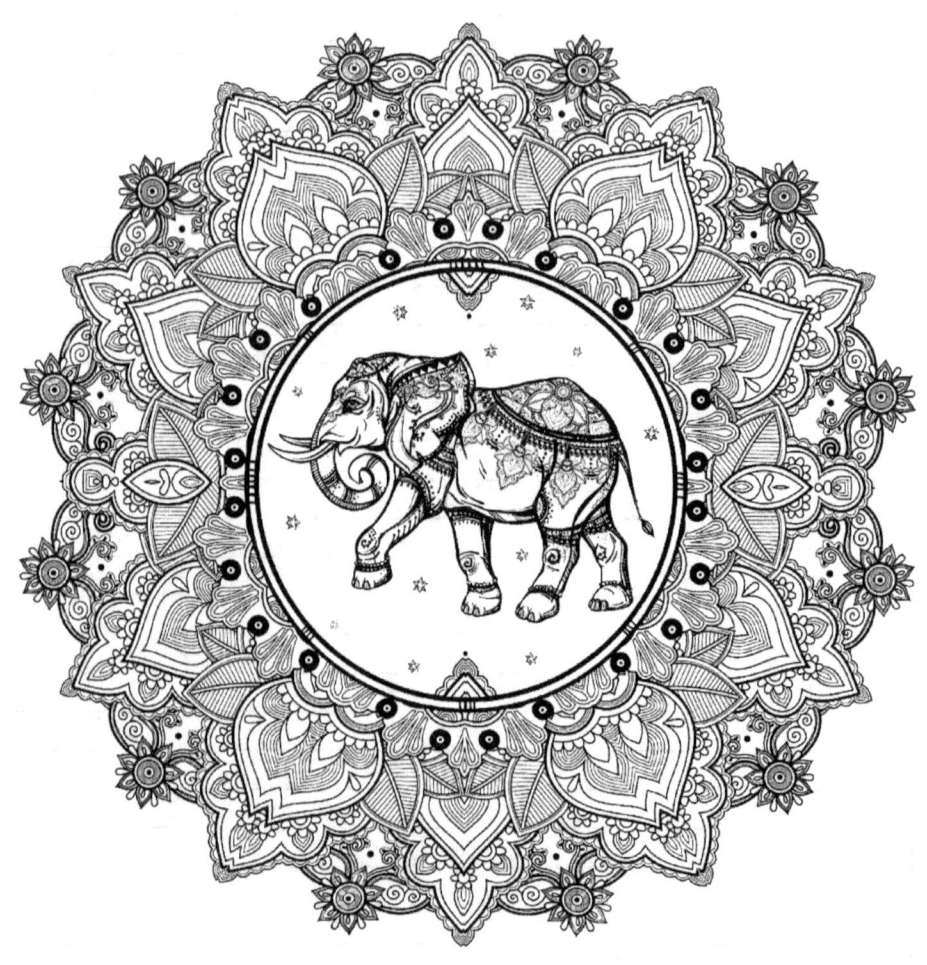

"Anger is the ultimate destroyer of peace of mind." Dalai Lama

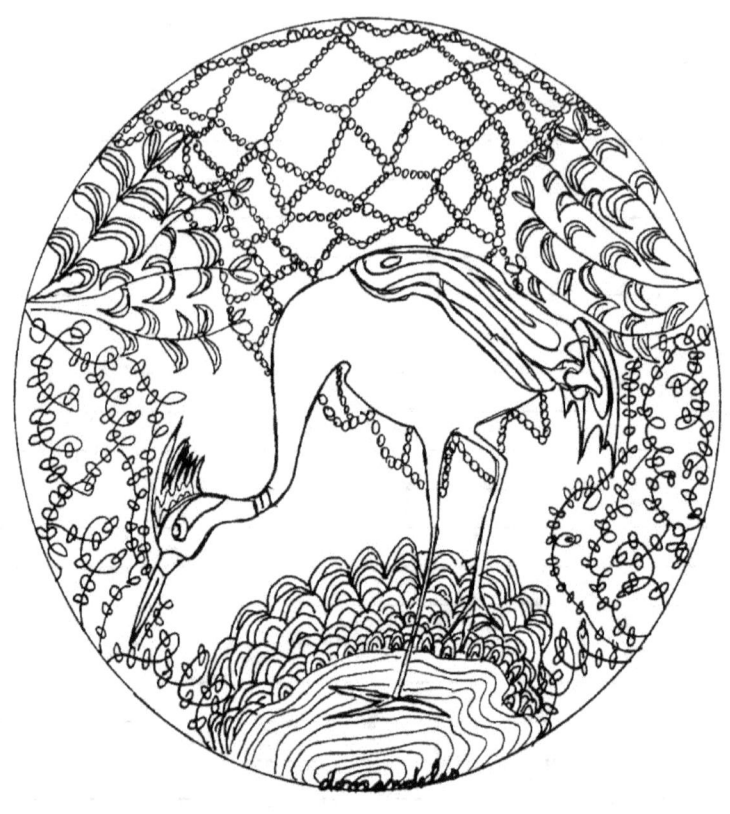

"Peace is the result of retraining your mind to process life as it is, rather than as you think it should be." —Wayne W. Dyer

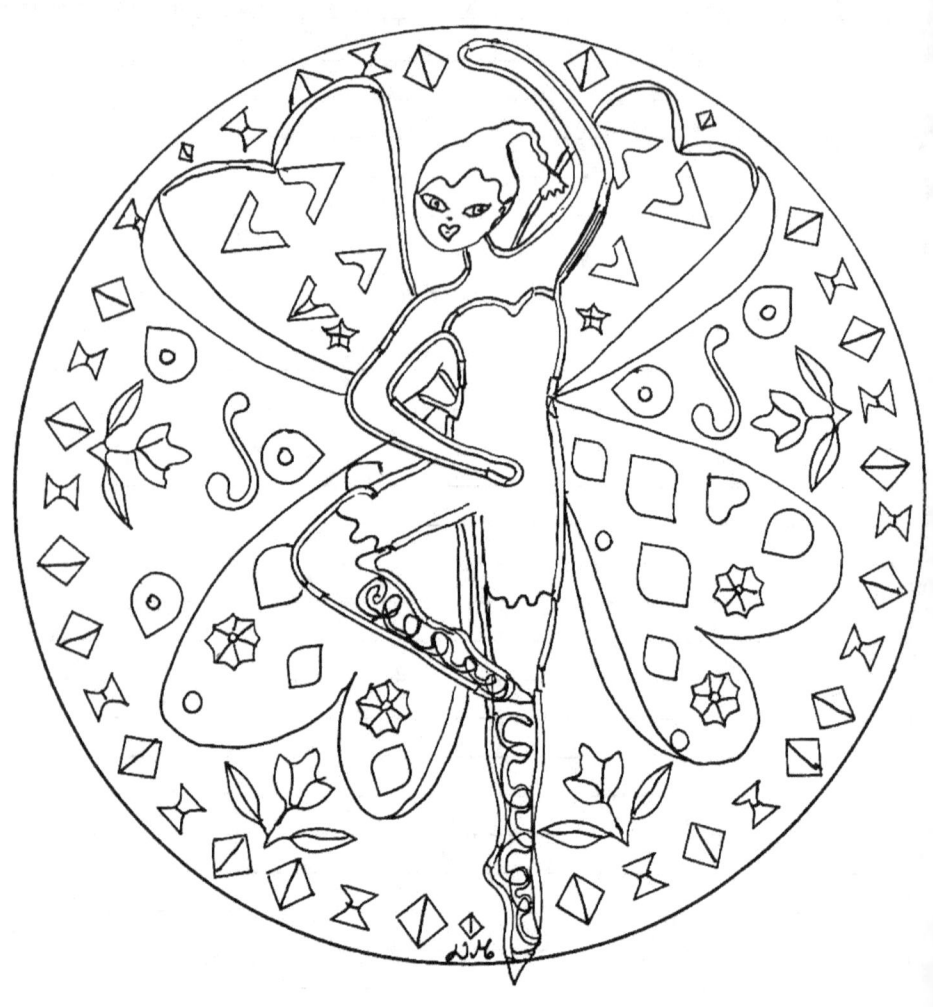

"Whoever values peace of mind and the health of the soul will live the best of all possible lives." Marcus Aurelius

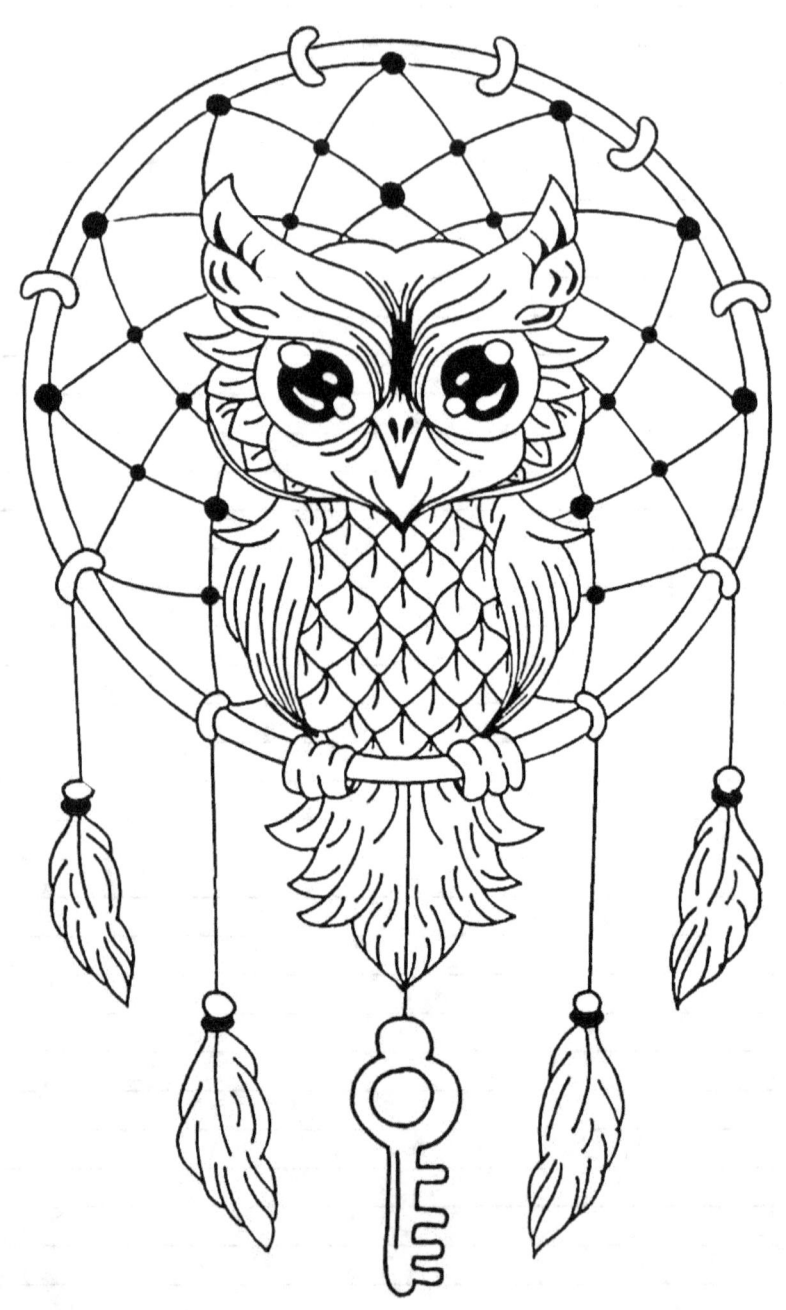

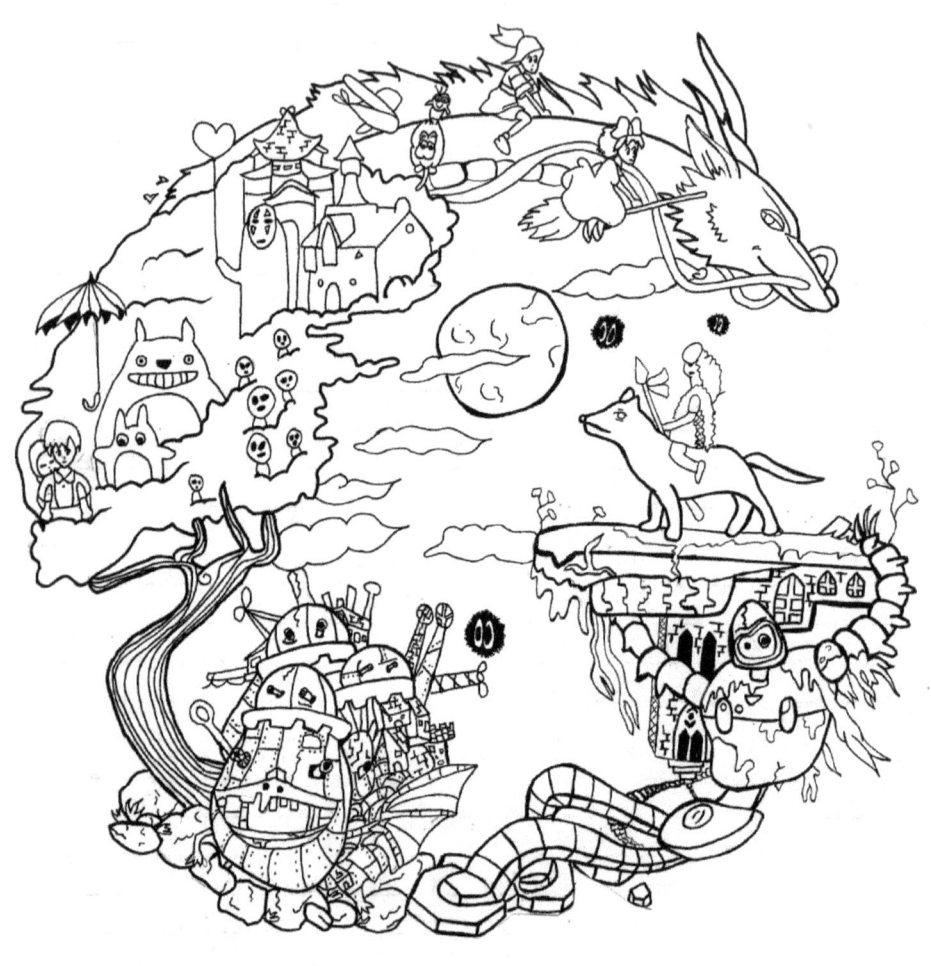

"Peace comes from within." Buddha

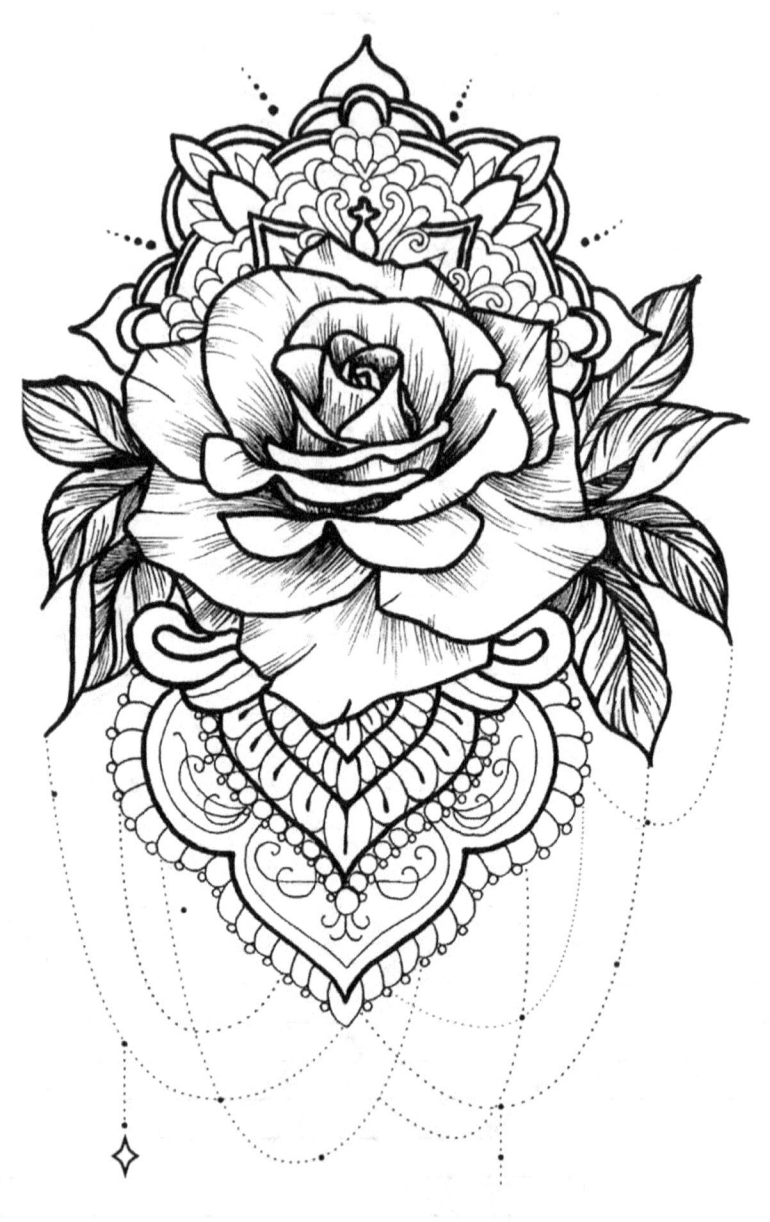

"If you want peace of mind, stop fighting with your thoughts." Anonymous

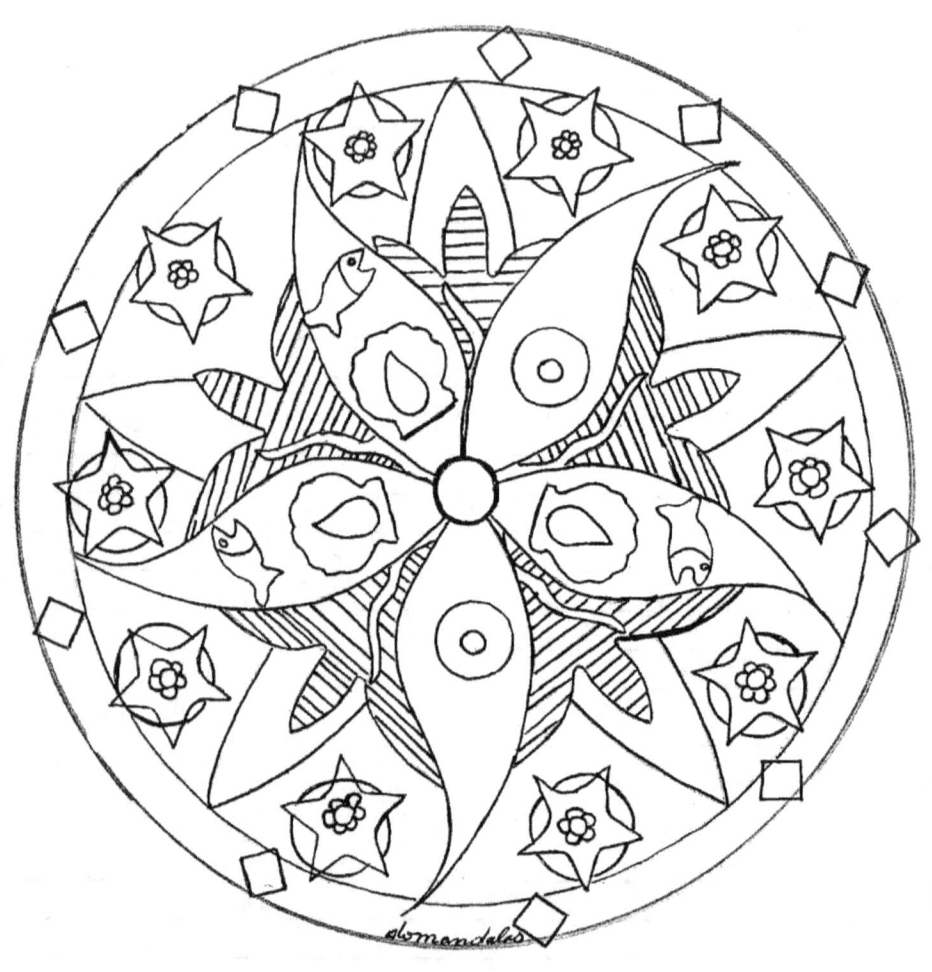

"Let go of the people who dull your shine, poison your spirit, and bring you drama." Anonymous

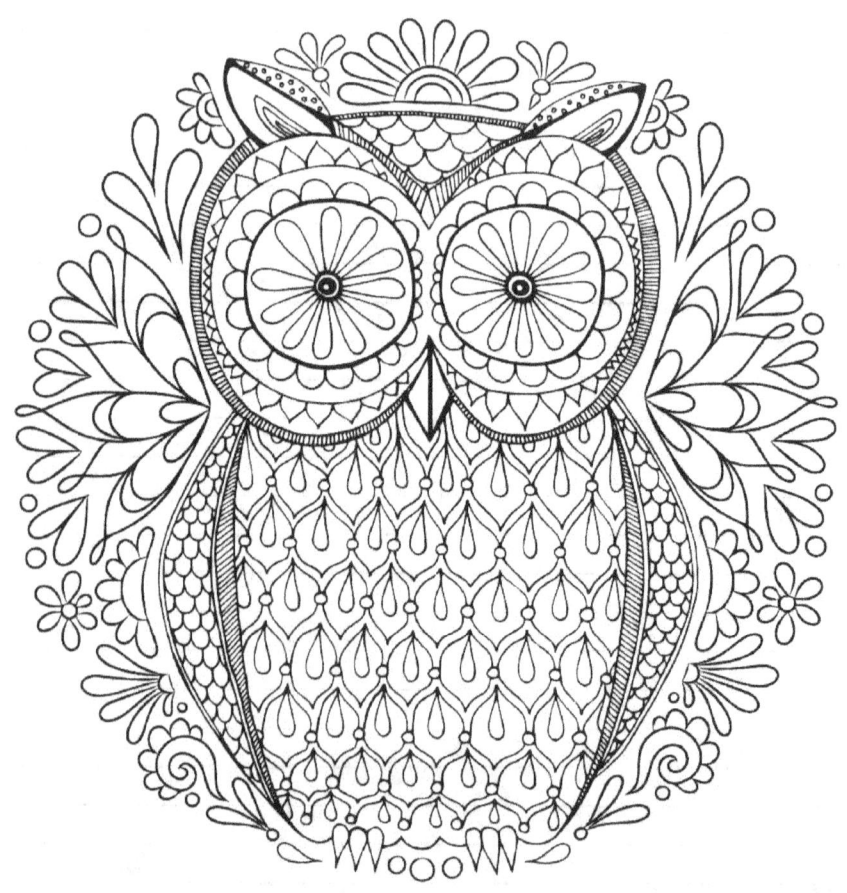

Gratitude is one of the sweet shortcuts to finding peace of mind and happiness inside." Anonymous

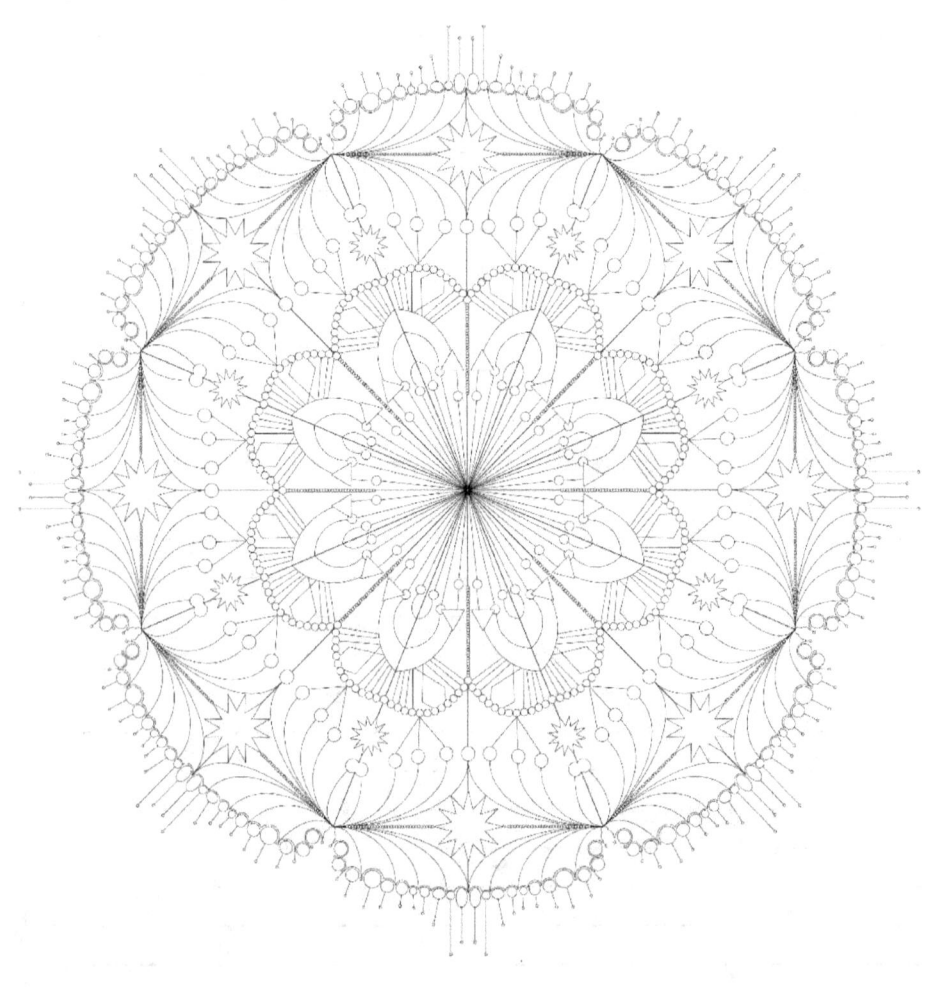

"Be ye angry, and sin not: let not the sun go down on your wrath,"
(Ephesians 4:26, KJV)

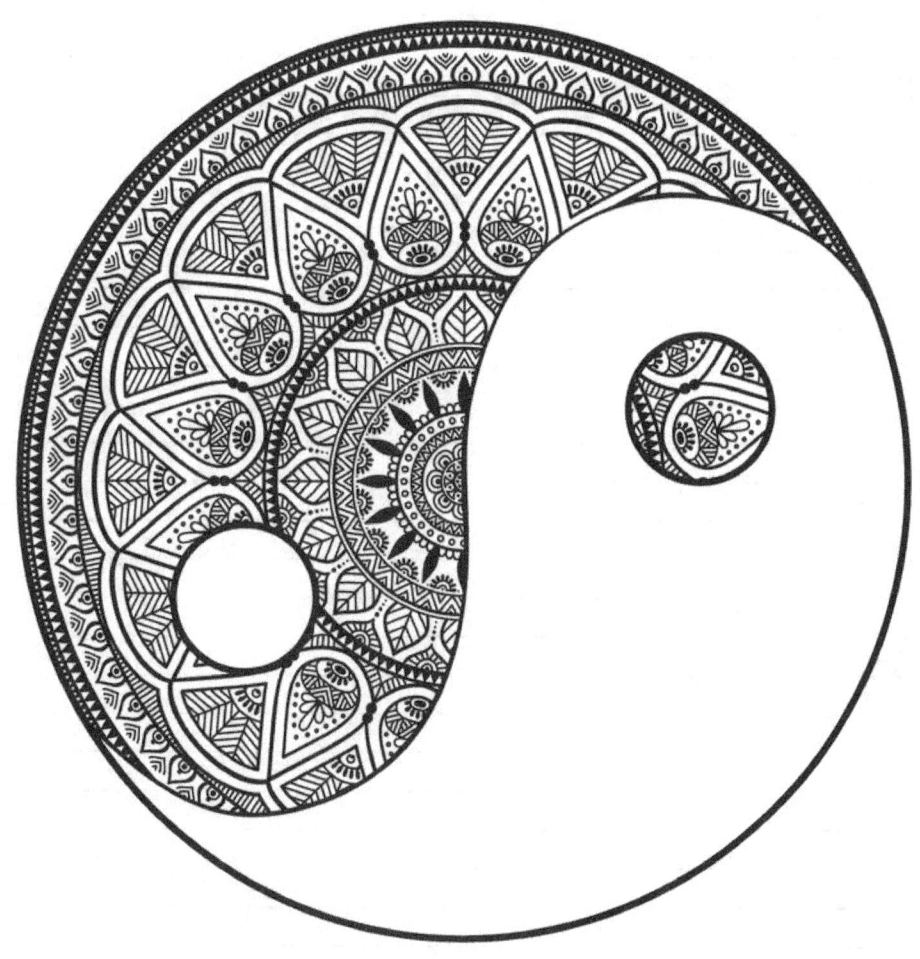

"Peace I leave with you, my peace I give unto you: not as the world giveth, give I unto you. Let not your heart be troubled, neither let it be afraid." (John 14:27, KJV)

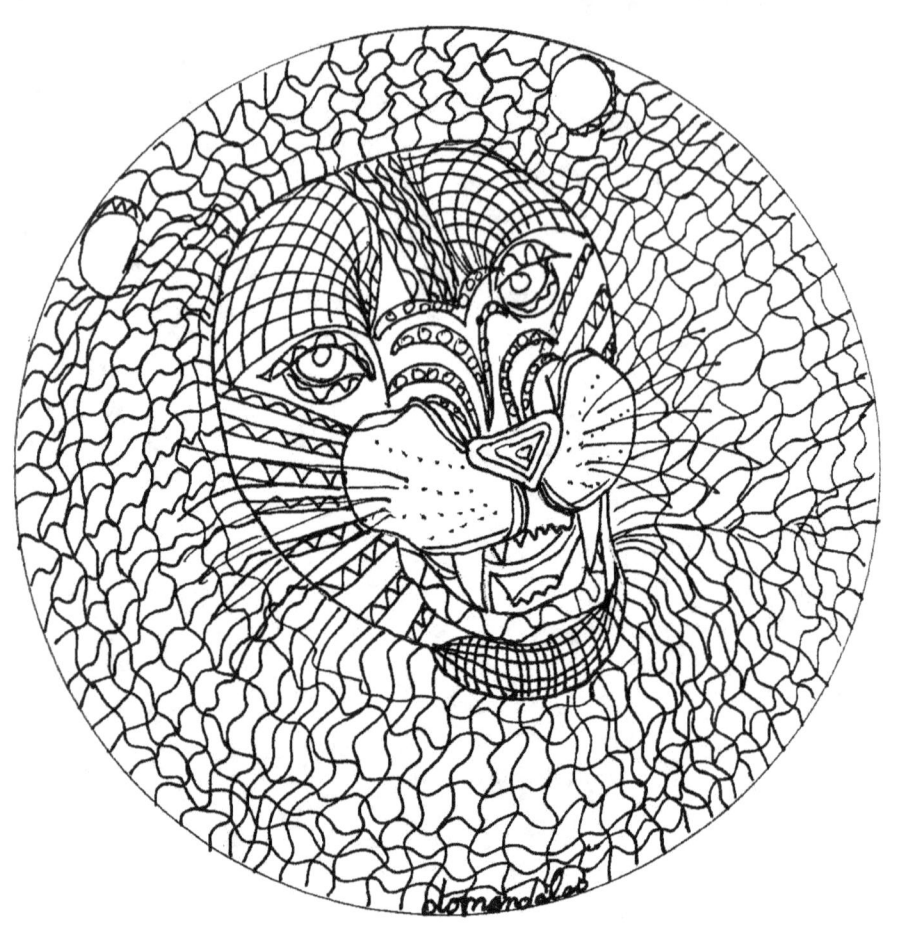

"Letting go of fears, troubles, and pain opens the door for peace and joy"
Stephinie R. Johnson

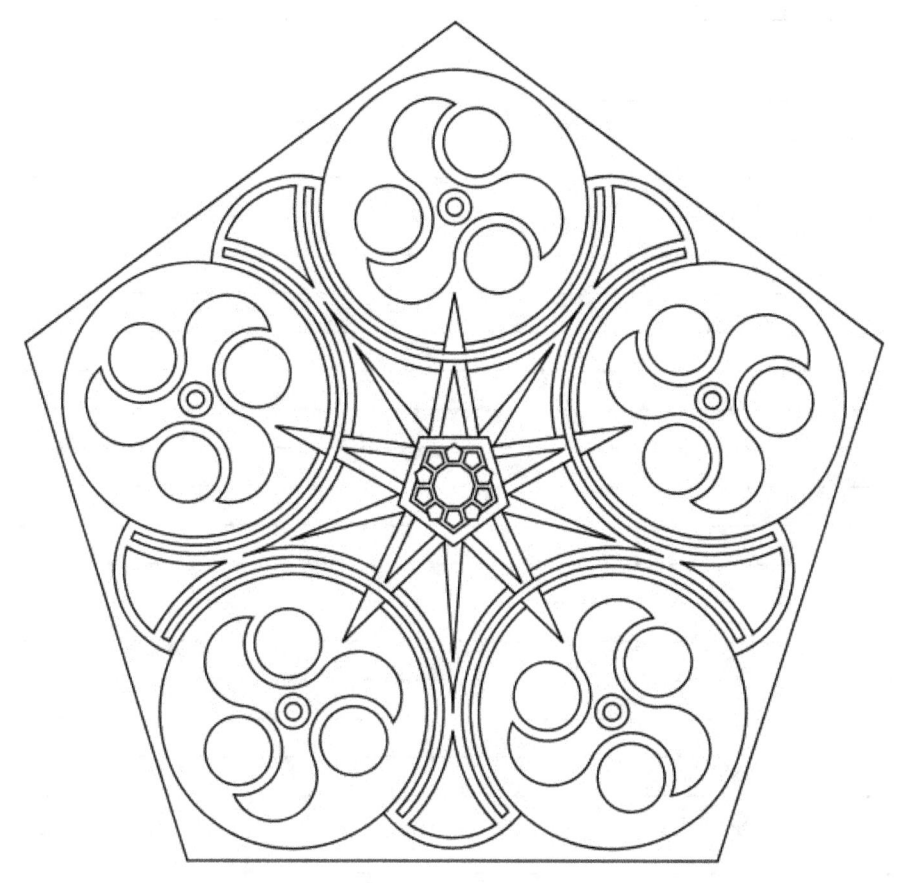

"We can never obtain peace in the outer world until we make peace with ourselves." Dalai Lama

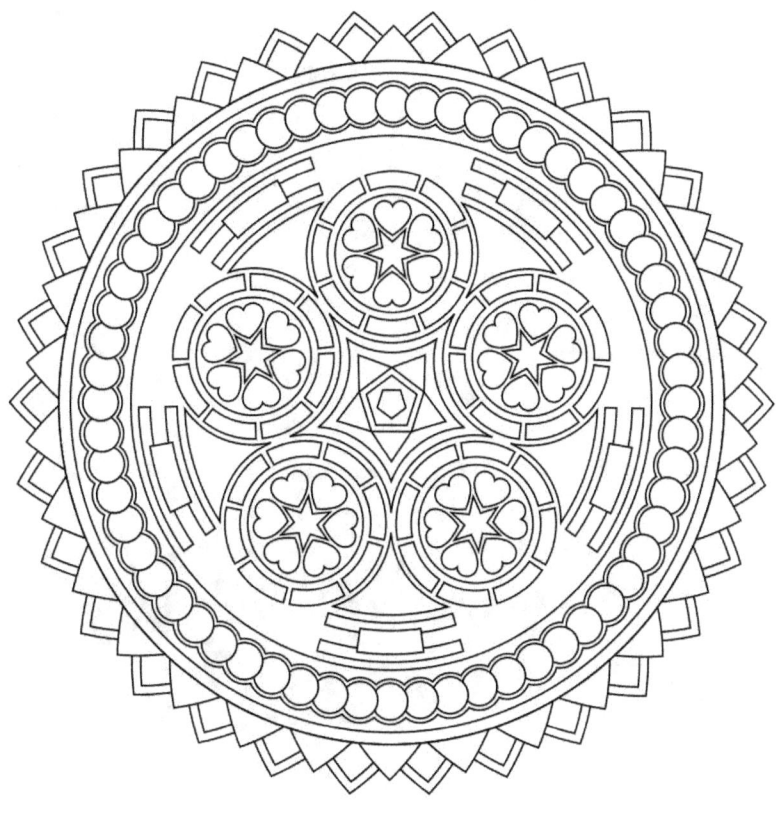

"You get peace of mind not by thinking about it or imagining it, but by quietening and relaxing the restless mind. Your nature is absolute peace. You are not the mind. Silence your mind through concentration and meditation, and you will discover the peace of the spirit you are and have always been." Remez Sasson

MANDALAS FOR THE WORK PLACE

www.ingramcontent.com/pod-product-compliance
Lightning Source LLC
Chambersburg PA
CBHW071839200526
45169CB00020B/1890